Making Lemonade with Georgia Grace
Edited by Eileen Sweeney
2018
Philadelphia, PA

Making Lemonade

with Georgia Grace

by Kelly Conway

Edited by Eileen Sweeney

Photo credit: Pet Imagery by Lauren Kaplan Photography

Dedications

Dedicated to Jim & Maureen Conway.
Thank you for loving and supporting us through our various health issues. Your love has helped to get us through many a tough time. You taught me how to be a good pet parent and I will always be grateful.
We love you to the moon & back!

Also dedicated to the all of the Cavalier King Charles Spaniels lovers in The Cavalier Brigade and the Cavalier Syringomyelia Army. Your support has been such a huge part of our lives. Georgia and I appreciate it more than words can say.

A big thank you to my neighbors Gina Altieri & Sharon St. John for loving Georgia & taking care of her when I couldn't. Your friendship means so much!

To Sam & Toby for loving me, & Maggie for showing me a special needs pet is worth fighting for.

To Dr. Daniel Silverberg, Dr. Cynthia Graves, & Dr. Leslee Feaster for putting up with my neurotic self and for helping to make Georgia's life as healthy & happy as can be.

And finally, dedicated to Quincy Rose, Lola Soprano, Isabella Rossilini, Georgia Grace, Milo James, & Jaxson Teller for making me a mommy.

Foreword

A lemon is used to describe an item that is defective. When I was a kid, my family had a car that was a lemon. I remember it always stalled every time my mom made a right hand turn. That car was frustrating and a money pit.

As an adult, I also purchased a lemon, but mine wasn't a car. It was a dog. A dog that some would also say is defective, frustrating, and a money pit. I was told this dog wouldn't live past three-years old, and I should put her to sleep because she would never have a normal life. Everyone had an opinion on what I should do about my beautiful, but chronically-ill Cavalier King Charles Spaniel. I listened to some things and ignored many others. In the end, I followed my gut. I decided that if I had a lemon, I was going to make lemonade, because Georgia Grace is the sweetest lemon around. This is her story...

Chapter 1: Puppyhood

Look at this cute puppy! It's me when I was 3 weeks old. My name was Nellie, and I was born on an Amish farm in Schuylkill County, Pennsylvania on April 19, 2009. I am a Tri-color Cavalier King Charles Spaniel. That is a pretty big name for such a little dog. I was one of three puppies that my mom wanted to meet when she was looking for a puppy. I knew she would pick me. Honestly, how could she resist?

Nellie

Well, in reality, Mommy almost resisted me. She was originally interested in my sister Nicki and needed some convincing that I was supposed to be her dog. So while Mommy played with Nicki, I kept biting her fingers, licking her face, and crawling all over her lap. All of this "convincing" was exhausting, so I curled up on Mommy's lap and fell asleep. Mommy looked down at me and fell in love. She told me that my name would be Georgia Grace. Isn't that the most beautiful name ever? Here are some pictures of the first time we met. Can you feel the love?

Mommy brought me home four weeks later. My new home had lots of fun toys and fancy clothes. Mommy taught me how to do lots of fun tricks and she told me I was the smartest puppy in the whole-wide world! I was a happy, playful and a perfect angel... Well, maybe I was a tad bit naughty. Tricolor Cavaliers are known for their naughtiness. I just couldn't help it! I was born this way!

Mommy also said I was beautiful. What do you think?

I was a happy and care-free puppy. I had a boyfriend, named Bentley, and we played together all day long. I might have been small, but I had a BIG attitude! My two big sisters, Lola and Isabella were harder to convince that I was likable. Lola seemed to like me some of the time, but Isabella didn't like any other animals, including Lola. She would bop me on the head and Lola would help me chase her away. Lola was a good big sister. We were a happy family!

Lola was my protector

Isabella tolerated me. She loved Mommy, so she shared the bed with me.

One of the few photos of all three of us together. Isabella didn't like me or Lola, so this was as close as she would get to us.

Chapter 2: Becoming a Warrior

Around my second birthday, things started to change. I began rubbing my head and snout so much that I would knock the cushions off of the couch. I eventually rubbed all the hair off my face in some spots. My veterinarian said I had allergies and mommy started giving me medicine. This went on for about 6 months until one day, I really didn't feel good and refused to be outside. I didn't want to go for walks or play with my friends. All I wanted to do was lie on the floor and sleep. Mommy was scared because I stopped being a happy and carefree dog.

Even my sister Lola noticed I was sick. She never played with me and normally, if I went near her, she'd run away and hiss at me. All of a sudden, Lola was my shadow. If I was lying on the floor or the couch, she was lying near me. Lola stayed by me at all times and would wake mommy in the middle of the night if I was crying out in pain. Mommy knew something was wrong the day Lola let me sleep with my head on her back. Lola didn't like anyone touching her, but she didn't move while I slept. She made me feel safe. If Lola was being nice to me, then something was really wrong. Mommy knew Lola's cat intuition was never wrong and she had to do something to help me feel better.

MRI day. August, 2011

Mommy researched Cavalier King Charles Spaniels breed diseases and found something called Syringomyelia. Syringomyelia is a neurological disease that can be caused by a malformation of the skull (Chiari Malformation). This abnormality in my skull presses on my brain and causes spinal cord fluid to leak out of my spine. This forms air pockets that are called syrinxes. It's a very painful and progressive disease. Mommy knew I had this disease because I had all of the symptoms.

The next thing I knew, I had an appointment with a neurologist at a big veterinary hospital in Philadelphia. My diagnosis of Syringomyelia was confirmed after an MRI. The neurologist prescribed medication for me and said a prognosis was hard to predict. She told my mommy that I might not make it past age 3 because the disease is painful, unpredictable, and difficult to control. They gave my mommy very little hope that things would be okay. I was a very sick and very sad girl. Mommy was very sad, too.

When I came home from the hospital, my friend Gauge was waiting for me. Gauge was also sick with degenerative myelopathy, but all he wanted to do was comfort me. He was my neighbor and always made me happy. Mommy carried me over to Gauge. He sniffed and licked my ears for the longest time. He made me smile on a very sad and scary day.

Gauge died when I was three years old and I still miss him so much. He taught me cool things like how to knock on my neighbor's door to beg for food. I still do this because Gauge taught me how. I'm lucky my neighbors think it is cute. Mommy always thought it was cute when Gauge knocked on our door, too. My sister Isabella didn't think it was cute and she used to chase him out of the house! Man that Isabella was a tough cookie.

It took almost 6 months to get my Syringomyelia under control.

Some days I felt good.

Other days, I felt bad.

Syringomyelia is very painful at times. It makes me feel sick and sad.

In November, 2011, I began falling down and had trouble walking up stairs. Mommy thought my Syringomyelia was advancing and rushed me back to the neurologist. It turned out it wasn't my neurological disease causing me to fall. I had another problem called hip dysplasia. Hip dysplasia is a painful heredity disease caused by abnormal development of the hips, which leads to joint deterioration and arthritis. Mommy cried again. The doctor prescribed an anti-inflammatory medication, in addition to my three Syringomyelia medications and sent us on our way.

Living with two painful, chronic diseases was hard. Mommy was worried that she couldn't give me a comfortable life. She knew she had to find something besides medicine to ease my pain. Then she heard about Dr. Graves, a veterinarian who practiced holistic medicine based on the principles of Tao. Dr. Graves turned out to be our angel. She prescribed Chinese herbs, acupuncture, and cannabinoids to help me feel better. Guess what? It worked!!! I started to feel better!! Acupuncture is one of my most favorite things in the world. I can't wait to go! All mommy has to say is, "Let's go see Dr. Graves!" and I run to the car. I love her and I love how acupuncture makes me feel. After a few months of acupuncture, I started to run and play again!

Acupuncture makes very happy!

Over the next few years, I was diagnosed with more illnesses. Some related to the Cavalier King Charles Spaniel breed, and others just bad luck. By age 6, I was living with Syringomyelia, hip dysplasia, luxating patellas (my kneecaps move), arthritis, chronic dry eye syndrome (I don't make tears anymore and mommy keeps them lubricated), and chronic ear and eye infections from head rubbing caused by Syringomyelia. It's a lot to manage, but Mommy made it all work. I had bad days, at times, but overall I was a happy and well-behaved dog. Ok, ok, I admit it. I was still pretty naughty most of the time. I ate computer cords, shoes, and stole all the food I could find. If I couldn't find food in my house, I just knocked on the neighbor's door and they would give me food. I finally realized that I was a lot bigger than Lola and Isabella now and I could boss them around. Life was pretty sweet!

Mommy figured if I was healthy enough to act naughty that things were going okay. I live with painful illnesses that would topple the strongest of men, but I never complained. Mommy says I am brave and a fighter. I was Wonder Woman for Halloween one year because mommy said I am a superhero, too. If I only had Wonder Woman's powers: I'd use them to fight for more doggie snacks!!

Chapter 3: Eight is not so Great

Things were going really well for a while. Anytime I went to the vet for a check up mommy would hold her breath while they listened to my heart. Cavaliers are known to have bad hearts and most of us end up with heart disease. Right before my 8th birthday, the vets heard a murmur. I had to see a new vet, a cardiologist. He listened to my heart and I had to take a test called an echocardiogram. This test showed that I had two leaking heart valves. Most cavaliers have only their mitral valve leak. I am an overachiever, so I also have a leaky tricuspid valve, too.

Mommy was so sad, but she never cries in front of me any more. She knows it upsets me when she cries, so she just smiled and pet my head while my cardiologist told her about my chronic valvular disease. I knew she was sad, but she kissed me and told we would be fine. You know what? We were fine. Nothing really changed for 9 months.

November of 2017 ended up being a pretty scary time for us. I was really thirsty all the time. I lost a lot of weight and felt so very sick. Mommy was pretty sure I had diabetes. It turns out I do have it, but in true Georgia Grace fashion, I had a complication from diabetes called diabetic ketoacidosis. This complication is so serious that I had to be hospitalized immediately because it is deadly. I had to spend 4 days in a hospital over the Thanksgiving holiday. Mommy didn't go to see my grandparents because the veterinarians said I might not survive the treatment due to my leaky heart. Grammy and Grandpop live far away and mommy didn't want me to be alone. She would come to visit me, and all I did was sleep on her or sit by her purse. Mommy was confused, but soon realized I sat by the purse because I knew she would take that when she left. I was determined to leave when that purse left, too! When the vet tech carried me back to my crate, I cried for mommy because all I wanted was to be home with her. I know that mommy cried, too, but she didn't let me see her do it.

The third day in the hospital a veterinarian gave Mommy the first sign of hope. She said she was "cautiously optimistic" that I would get better. I knew I wanted to go home, so I tried my best to get better.

I did what the doctors wanted and I slowly started to feel better. I was released from the hospital on Day 4 at 9:30 pm. Mommy was so happy. I was happy too, but I was also very tired. In the hospital, I had to sleep in a crate. I have a crate at home, but the door is always open. I'm not a sleep-in-a-crate-with-the-door-closed kind of gal. I barked at the vet techs and they would let me out, but I snored so loudly that the other animals weren't sleeping, so I had to go back in my crate. First thing I did at home was climb on the couch and get comfy. I tried to watch some TV, but I couldn't keep my eyes open. It was so good to be home.

I now had to have two glucose test and two shots of insulin a day. Mom was nervous, but I wasn't. I had faith she would take good care of me....and guess what? I was right!

Diabetes was a lifestyle change for me. I could no longer have snacks and it took mom a while to get my blood glucose under control. I didn't make it easy....I like, no I LOVE my treats. I became obsessed with food. Mom would put it down and I would inhale it as fast as I could. This caused me to get something called "bloat." It is a deadly condition in which gas built up and made big balloon-like bubble in my belly. It was so big, that the doctors couldn't hear my heart murmur because it was stopping the blood flow to my heart! Luckily Mommy recognized what happened quickly and rushed me to the emergency room. I was so unhappy that I had to spend another night in the hospital. Lucky for me, mommy caught everything in time and I didn't need surgery. Most dogs have their stomach flip! My leaky heart valves, Syringomyelia and my diabetes made me really hard to manage, but I got treatment really fast and it saved my life. Bloat could be deadly, but like a warrior, I fought back again. Take that bloat!

Even when I am sick, I still manage to smile. Mommy says that is why she fights so hard for me. I am so full of life!

Now my days are filled with blood glucose checks and two shots of insulin. I also take 16 pills a day. I don't mind. Mom puts them in yummy treats. Mmmmmm....I love treats! This medicine stuff isn't so bad. I don't really mind the shots. Mommy is pretty good at giving them so most of the time, I don't feel it. My heart got worse, too. Now I take big pills for my leaky heart valves. I don't mind. They taste yummy! A treat is a treat in my book!!

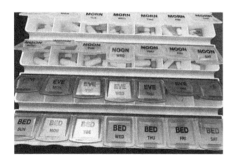

My pill sorter holds 112 pills for the week.

This is my diabetes supplies. Mommy keeps them organized.

My medical needs are a lot to handle for one person, but mom works really hard to make sure I get what I need. People often feel bad for me when they hear about all of my illnesses, but Mommy tells them not to feel bad. I am a happy girl. Mommy said since we never know what the future holds, we will make sure we live life to the fullest. Life would be filled with adventure, fun, and lots of love. My mommy focuses on living my life and not worrying about what we can't control. We have a lot of fun together. Let me tell you about it....

Chapter 4: Celebrate Life

The good life begins with making each moment count! Every year my birthday is a major event. Mom didn't know how many birthdays I would have, so she decided to make the most out of each and every one of them. The kids in the neighborhood and my family all help me celebrate. These are pictures from my first through sixth birthdays. I love wearing my party hat and getting puppy birthday cakes!

I'm making my "not impressed" face in my 6th birthday picture? I crack myself up!

My 7th birthday was on Easter,
so I got to celebrate with my
Grandparents. They spoil me
so I got to sit at the table!

On my 8th birthday, I was
annoyed because my
kitten brothers kept trying
to steal my birthday hat!

My 9th birthday was fun. Like
my new hat? My kitten brothers
destroyed my other birthday
hat, so Mommy bought me this
one. I look pretty cute, right? I
know I haven't talked about my
brothers. I'll get to them later.

Birthdays with my dog and people friends are the BEST!

33

Chapter 5: A Passion for Fashion

I am a fashionista and I love to dress up, especially for Halloween!! I help pass out candy and get lots of pets from kids who come to see me every year. Which costume is your favorite?

Halloween 2017

#MakeASceneContest
#PetCo
#Georgiathecavalier

I've won some costume contests and have been featured
on lots of websites, in books, and even some TV shows!

GEORGIA & LOLA
The early settlers had to set their differences aside and learn to get along.

TMZ's St. Paddy's Day
Photo Contest -- WINNER!

THE REST...

CLICK TO SEE THE PHOTOS ▸

TMZ.com

The tribe has spoken -- and the adorable Party Pooch was the blarney best in our annual **St. Paddy's Photo Contest** -- scoring the **$250 pot-o-gold** and some great gifts from TMZ!

I love being a fashionista!

As you can see, I have an outfit for every occasion and a coat for every season!

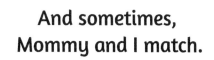

And sometimes, Mommy and I match.

Chapter 6: Oh the Places You Will Go

Mommy and I love to travel. Even a visit to see my Grandparents is a two-hour drive. I love the car and even have my very own car seat! I am a bit naughty, so I do try to climb out of it to see where we are going!

I make a pretty good copilot! I even know how to put the windows down so I can feel some air on my face. Sadly, Mommy knows how to lock the windows, so I don't get to do that often. I love meeting people and animals, so I am always up for a road trip.

I love the New Jersey Shore. There are these things called Seagulls that look delicious! I keep trying to catch them, but mom says I'm not allowed to eat them. I guess they have too many carbs for my diabetes.

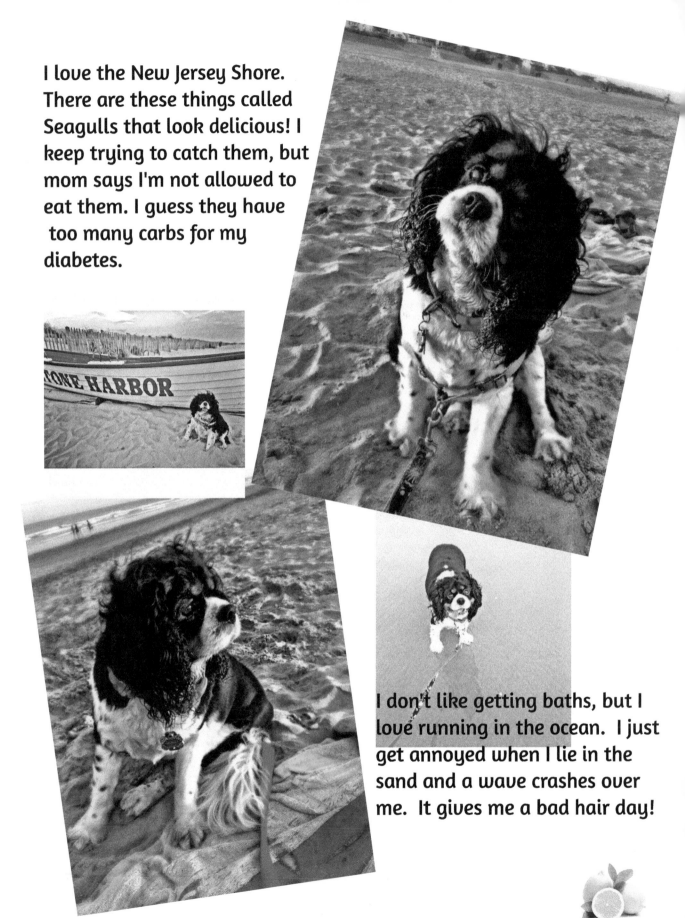

I don't like getting baths, but I love running in the ocean. I just get annoyed when I lie in the sand and a wave crashes over me. It gives me a bad hair day!

I love going on adventures with my mom. I get to meet lots of people and dogs. My health issues and getting older make walking around like I used to a bit harder. So mommy bought me a stroller. I love it! It puts me at the perfect height to get pet by all the people we meet. I feel like a queen!

Mommy loves my stroller, not only does it hold her coffee, but it's the perfect accessory for my Halloween costumes! Have I mentioned that I am an "award winning dog"? I've won the best in talent event at the annual Philadelphia Mutt Strut two years in a row! You see; I'm not just beautiful, I'm super smart, too. Oh, and I won best costume for my "Barkfest at Tiffany" costume. I looked pretty good that day if I do say so myself. The stroller helps me attend fun events like the Mutt Strut. I don't get as tired and still get to socialize and have fun. It's perfect!

My favorite trip was to an event called, "CAVAPALOOZA". It's a gathering of Cavalier King Charles Spaniel owners and their dogs. It was in West Virginia. I got to meet cavaliers in all different colors! I was so surprised when everyone knew my name. I felt like a Superstar!

Here I am with Bad Boy Beau!

Ollie, Maggie & Harley Halliday! Aren't they cute? Can you see me in the back?

The Newmans with Anna Lee Rose & Maggie Mae. I was so excited to meet them! Mommy shows me their pictures all the time. They are divas just like me!

44

I smiled just about the entire time I was at Cavapalooza! I loved meeting all my Cavalier Cousins!

Photo credit: David Torrance

I was especially excited to meet Jamie. Mommy said he is blind and deaf Cocker Spaniel. People seemed to want to take a lot of pictures of the two of us because we have "special needs." I'm not sure what that means, but I thought he was very handsome.

The only time I stopped smiling was when Mommy told me that I couldn't take Harper Grace home with us. Mommy tried to "steal" her for me but wasn't successful. I thought Harper Grace & Georgia Grace would make a good team!   We remain facebook friends and I hope to get the chance to sniff her cuteness again someday.

Harper Grace

I had so much fun with all the dogs and people that I slept really well each night. I love sleeping in bathrooms. The floors are cool and my snores echo so mom can enjoy them while she (tries to) sleep! Cavapalooza was the best weekend of my life!

Photo credit: Pet Imagery by Lauren Kaplan Photography

Chapter 7: So far Nine is fine

I turned 9 this year. We celebrated my birthday weekend by going to a "Cavalier Meet Up". It was a fun day to meet lots of rescued Cavaliers. I got to see some of my friends from Cavapalooza again, too.

Mommy was so proud of me!

Our friends Melissa, Parker, Abigail, and Tucker

Oliver joined Parker, Abigail, Tucker, and I for treats!

I took a test, too. I was a bit nervous because I didn't even study!! It was called the Canine Good Citizen Test. It determines how good my manners are and if my mommy is a responsible owner. I took it about 2 years ago, and I failed the "separation" part where mommy has to leave me for 3 minutes. I don't like to be away from my mommy. Mommy's friend Melissa encouraged us to try it again, and guess what? I passed!! I even got a blue ribbon!

Earning my CGC ribbon was great, but mommy thought I could do even better. She signed me up for the therapy dog test, and guess what?? I passed that test, too! I am now an official therapy dog and can visit schools, nursing homes, and hospitals. I even got to go to work with mommy! She is a speech language pathologist and works in a school with lots of amazing kids. Here are some pictures of me with some of new friends! They were all so nice and cuddly!

I love being a therapy dog! It's a lot of fun even though it's serious work! I snored the whole way home in the car. As you can see, I am a very busy dog, but mommy makes sure I don't overdo things because of my chronic illnesses.

Being therapeutic is exhausting.....zzzzzzz

Besides being busy at work and traveling, I also like to have relax and have fun! I love snuggling with mommy.

I really love going on walks no matter what the weather is like. Mommy is not a fan of cold and rainy walks, but she takes me every day no matter what!

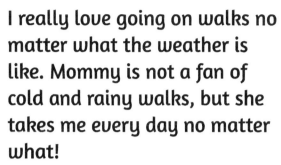

I love spending time with my human friend Maddie. She always pets me and puts leaves in my hair. I also have a pack with Darla, Cupcake, & Bailey. We love hanging out. Sitting in my yard is one of my most favorite things to do. Aren't my friends cute??

What I love most of all is my family. My Grammy and Grandpop treat me like a human grandkid.

I love when Grammy rubs my belly and gives me snuggles. She also cooks me yummy food and makes me feel so special.

Grandpop and I watch Western movies together. I run to the TV to bark and chase the the horses and cows away. I run back to Grandpop and he says, "Atta girl Georgie!" We have fun, especially when he drops crumbs on the floor. Yummy!

I even kind of, sort of, love my little brothers even though they can be pests. You see Lola and Isabella crossed something called the "Rainbow Bridge". Mommy was afraid I would be lonely home alone all day. She took me to meet some kittens and two little guys seemed to really like me. I was still missing my sister Lola, so it took me a while to warm up to the "boys". I don't like to snuggle with them, but I do like to chase them around the house. I especially like it when they help me get food off of the table. Milo and Jaxson come in handy when I can't reach stuff!

Although Milo and Jaxson are trouble makers, they keep me active. Jax tries to stop me from going upstairs to steal his food, and Milo likes to pull my coat off so I can't leave him. Mommy spoils all of us.

Most of all, I love my Mommy. I love to wake her up early on Saturday mornings so she can take me to Dunkin Donuts. Mom gets her coffee and I used to get a munchkin. Now that I have diabetes, I can't have munchkins anymore, but I get a healthy delicious treat instead. It's all good!

I love all the things Mommy and I do together. We have so much fun! The only thing I don't like is when we are away from each other for too long. We are a team and just belong together. I think Mommy would agree. She loves me even when I sneeze on her during a photo shoot.

    Photo credit: Pet Imagery by Lauren Kaplan Photography

So that is my story about living with chronic illness. As you can see, I have a GREAT life! I hope you liked hearing about it. I really liked telling it to you! Now I'm going to go sit on top of my hill and soak up the sun. Life is good!

Photo credit: Pet Imagery by Lauren Kaplan Photography

In my words:

I've been living with multiple chronic illnesses for over 20 years, including rheumatoid arthritis. When Georgia was diagnosed with her first illness, Syringomyelia, I was devastated. I live my life in pain and was determined my sweet, funny, smart little dog was not going to live like that, too. I wasn't given much hope at the time of her first diagnosis. Little did I know that my knowledge of chronic illnesses and Georgia's unbreakable will would allow her to see nine birthdays, and hopefully many more. I have contemplated euthanasia twice over the years when things got really bad, but new treatments have helped us overcome many challenges. Georgia, like me, has good and bad days, but overall, her quality of life is really good. She is a very happy dog.

I originally wanted a dog to help me be more active and mobile. I faithfully take Georgia for daily walks to keep my body moving. Ironically, our arthritis makes us walk with similar gaits and the similarities don't end there. I take 12 pills a day, she takes 16 pills a day. I take one shot a month, she takes two shots a day. We both have skin diseases that can't seem to be cured, and sadly, we both struggle with pain management. The similarities are endless. It's obvious to me that she was meant to be mine.

Our worst time was when we both broke our legs two days apart. We both needed to have surgery. I left Georgia with my parents for 3 long months because I couldn't take care of her. Each night I would FaceTime my parents just to see her. I was told she would hear the phone ring and would walk over to whomever was holding it to "chat" with me. I missed her terribly and still remember the joy I felt when she came home. Separations have never been easy on either of us.

Although caring for Georgia can be difficult and stressful at times, I would never trade a moment with her for the world. Her genuine love of life and quirky personality makes her endearing to all who meet her. Georgia lives with diseases that would topple most people, yet she never complains. In many ways, she inspires me to be better, try harder, and never give up the fight with my own health. Her purpose on this earth is to love and be loved and she does it well. Lucky for me, I am the one who gets to love her the most.

A portion of every book sold will support Nonni's Fund. This fund helped me when Georgia was hospitalized with diabetes. I will forever be grateful for their help.

Nonni's Fund

Nonni's Fund was created by a few special members of the Cavalier Brigade, an organization of friends who network to assist in the rescue of Cavalier King Charles Spaniels from critical and often horrific conditions. Nonni was a rescue herself directly from puppy mill in Missouri at the age of 7 when she no longer was a profitable breeder. She and her breeding mate, Bailey were offered for sale on Craig's List for a nominal fee.

Nonni lived on for three glorious years in love and the life she deserved. She died suddenly and quickly of a seizure. It was a devastating loss to all who had followed her rescue and her blossoming into a quirky, lively, bossy little girl. Because she exemplified so many mill mamas and the tough resiliency of the breed, a fund was started to help other mill mamas and rescues in need, hence Nonni's Fund.

Nonni continues to help from above. Although she had been debarked by the "millers", her voice can still be heard loud and clear in the good will that she spreads to the Cavaliers across the nation who are helped by the proceeds of Nonni's Fund.

Nonni's Mom

Thanks!!

This book would not have been possible without the help from the following people:

A HUGE thank you to Georgia's veterinarians, Dr. Daniel Silverberg and Dr. Leslee Feaster & all the staff at Township Line Animal Hospital for their loving care and guidance. Georgia loves you!

Photos by Kelly Conway. Other photos included by:
-Lauren Kaplan from Pet Imagery by Lauren Kaplan Photography, Philadelphia, PA
-David Torrance
-Rebecca Sheehan
-Carol O'Toole
-Dave Ziggy Derksen

Thanks to the following friends who allowed me to include their children and/or pets in Making Lemonade:

Friends with pets in Making Lemonade:
Gina, Nick, Nicholas & Sonny Alteri with Darla, Gauge,& Bentley.
(Special shout out to Lacey, their 18 year old rescue Maltese. Georgia and I love you, too!)
Betsy McGuire and Cupcake. Christine Carney and Bailey.
Melissa King and Parker, Abigail & Tucker. Melissa MacMullin and Oliver. Barbara & Bob Halliday and Ollie, Maggie, & Harley. Leeanne & Jim Newman with Maggie Mae & Anna Lee Rose. Brenda Maeder and Jamie. Kathy Hicks and Harper. Linda & Steve Ellis with Beau.

Friends with children in Making Lemonade:
Becky, Brendan, Michael, Conor, Dermot, & Fiona Sheehan. Lynn, Kevin, Sean, & Liam Murphy. Mia White, Pete Barnes & Maddie Barnes. Angela, John & Regent Walden. Jacklyn, Ben, Jared, & Jaden Lieberman.

For more info on Cavalier King Charles Spaniels and health issues, go to: Cavalier Health at http://www.cavalierhealth.org

Sometimes all you need is.....

The End

Lightning Source UK Ltd.
Milton Keynes UK
UKHW051951041021
391649UK00002B/184